# The Waterfall

Sarah Charnelle Morris

BookLeaf
Publishing

India | USA | UK

Made with ❤ on the BookLeaf Publishing Platform
www.bookleafpub.in
www.bookleafpub.com

# Dedication

This is for all who watched my waterfall. Those who dried my tears and those who were washed away.

# Preface

# Acknowledgements

# 1. One Tear I Cried

I knew you before
And you knew my name
Then I got lost in hope
And you in your game
Your world wasn't mine
Couldn't find your name
Hidden from sight
In some other plane
I imagined you there
How I hoped you to be
Though again we met
You couldn't meet me
You didn't see my world
So a memory you stayed
I a discarded pawn
In the game you played
As my heart was lost
Yours not for me
Your door wouldn't open
Though I had the key

Worse than this
You didn't look
I wasn't real
Enough for the book
So away I fade
Waving away from you
A ghost from the past
Something now untrue
I will live in my world
Now filled with my lies
Of how I'm over you
And everything is fine

# 2. Filtered Water

Storytime now
Lies
Hopes
Dreams
And never could-be's
Told, so one day they would
Somewhen its real
A script for us written
To run
To hide
To seek
A body singing a way
Home
Away we wander
With a wilder river in our hearts
The river will follow us now

# 3. Dehydration

The dry desert
The sun burns everything here
Kills as much life as it gives
Maybe more
Here we burn for the crime of existence
Born into this place
Fire ever around us
A well painted hell
No tears left to cry
Ever dried, but not the sadness
We wait
Calling for rains that won't come
Oceans of long ago still singing
The lost beach remembers
We remember
The flow of rivers
The waves of life
Nothing now
Just dust and stillness
Burning hot sand

We wait on the lost shore
Love once flowed here
This too into dust
A dehydrated people
Hardened
Blended with the sand and thorns
Some fleeing in search lost waves
Of lost moments and lost hope
Some remain knowing their place
Time for the raindance

# 4. The Fare Thee Well

Once there was a dragon
Not the largest of them all
But more cunning than the rest
And faster being small
He watched the other dragons
Swirling in the wind
But no one no where
Was ever fast as him
He also knew a secret
About how the rivers came
He tried to tell the others
But they kept to their games
So alone he went
To find the river's source
His heart beating fast
For it knew the course
Rivers seem to spring
Or come from clouds that fall
But this dragon knew the truth
He felt this his call

A hidden world behind
All the lies they tell
A giant magic land
Behind the veil of hell
A white-haired lovely woman
Bartered for their land
Each morning she rose
With new stones in hand
She traded them with a smile
For rain and wind and trees
And gave them to the dragon's world
To do with as they pleased
She loved them more than diamonds
She loved when they would fly
She knew they would get thirsty
And couldn't leave them dry
The dragon found her there
Just like she knew he would
She called for him you see
And knew that he was good
The dragon must carry forward
With her loving plan
Her time was nearing end
And she trust no man
The dragon ate her whole
So with him she could fly

He felt her in his soul
Never would they die

# 5. Rain Bucket

I think it strange
What we love
About women
The ones that keep us
The ones who loved us into the lives we lead
Oh the treasures they gave us
Like how to save the rain
And how to boil the water
How to hang the clothes to dry
Like what life can weather the desert sun
And how she laughed in that sun
Feeding plants in defiance of desert heat
A natural disorder
A rebellion
My grandmother
We will live
I will save the rain

# 6. Data Stream

Made of light and tomorrow
With winds of yesterday
The captain sailed forward
From the crowded bay
The plan was sure
The hope was strong
The ship was study
Yet his heart was wrong
In water such as these
There can be no doubt
Love knows something we forget
Its ever been the route
His journey brought him sharks
And pirates of all kinds
Waves as tall as towers
And fogs that made him blind
Lost so far at sea
A cracken grasp the ship
His time had come he felt
As the beast increased its grip

He would surely drown
The ship surely would be lost
He prepared to face death
The heart now ready for the cost
Suddenly awakened
By this massive threat
The captain grabbed his musket
Told the men to forget
Remeber your bravery mates
This beast is but a meal
Rip him limb from limb
Our lives he will not steal
The men began to slash and shoot
In a most ferocious fight
The beast finally relented
After long into the night
As the morning came
The captain ordered the repairs
His course now corrected
Never again scared
He felt the call again
To tomorrow's home
The wind with him again
His heart would never roam.
Ever true to course
Even through the night
The tomorrow he knew for them

Was worth every fight.

# 7. The Water Rises

Star walker
Light to light
Galaxy to galaxy
He fled
Escaping his fate
An eternal run
Death would claim him never
Nor would love
Unclouded
A vision held
A dream remembered
An enduring pursuit
Of a time long ago
Reality fading behind
Only forever before him
Or never
Time forgotten
No tomorrow
No today
Just the light

No home to find
No intention
Refusing what was
Unbearable suffering
He would shine for no more
Yet always had
The stars did not fall
They fled
Such is fate
It is
In spite of us
Without the light
They would see

# 8. The Red Ocean

Waves of suffering
True suffering
No cause
No answer
All we had when food was scarce
The kids were fed
The lies were told
The work was done
I had no hope
But we ran for our lives
Our lives
A game for children
Existence to some of us
All of us
But they wouldn't bear this lode
This weight
This wait
This gravity
The gravid earth
Ready

As were we
Yet so not
Birthing new worlds
Bloodshed
Tears
Same as any
Woe be to those
Woah be to those
We sang in red waters
We commanded these waters
We weathered these waters
From wine into water
We thirst no more
We will thirst no more

# 9. Lost Lake

He was a wave
Passing through me
Like water
Cool and light
Deep and terrifying
He slipped through my hands
They dried so quickly in the heat I call home
Leaving a wound I could not name
And tears that had no time to fall
Each time I swim now
I feel him
Like he is the water
Left haunted by that touch
A call to a home I won't have
A call to world I won't know
A glimpse
And I left searching
For something
For the lost lake

# 10. A Tall Drink of Water

How does the forest call my name
It lives so far from me
Perhaps from lives long ago
Maybe hiding all I need
The shade, the dance, the hidden things
Might wish to see me too
I forever hold the feeling
Of the things I though I knew
Perhaps a spirit calls to me
To carry him home to hide
Among the thickest trunks of trees
Or in caves just to the side
Perhaps I am one of them
Or soon will become
Never much a witch
But the dances look so fun
I want to hear the wind
Tell stories through the leaves
Each time they know just what to say
Perhaps it comes to me

I won't have to say a word
They will know my name
They let me stand tall as I can
And show me when to sway
To darkest forest my heart is called
When my mind forgets the way
To breath the air and know the earth
To feel alive again
To see the creatures wandering
And making some my friends
A deeper space than I usually find
On the roads I walk
I wish to live among the trees
Where no one has to talk
I cannot bear to say more
To those who cannot hear
I want the language of before
The invention of the year
So to the woods I will soon go
Forgive me when I leave
I love you still and always will
But I must let me breathe

# 11. Light River

How quickly we know one another
And forget as fast
The lies we tell the fear we hide
Covering all
Our names meet and explain
All that we ever were
But oh, the work of the world
Oh, the ways in which were pulled
How time carries us in different directions
How hardened hearts and winds of our mind
Can't bear it
So we know
But we are lost
A strange cruelty
A harder torture to endure
We can hide together
But our rage, our hurt
Not quite the shade we hoped for
Together, apart
Our moment passed

From this knowing how the rain does fall
Remember me
But there is nothing to forget
Having come to this
We now are

# 12. Roaring

Through the caves of monsters
And deep into the woods
The was once an ocean
Upon which no time stood
A man across the water
In a space time forgot
He waited for one like him
And this was just the spot
He could see all the people
Passing the days by
Knew he would know when
Didn't quite know why
He was where he was
And every one was there
He hoped someone like him
Wouldn't get too scared
He would call to them
From time to time
His people soon coming
He'd know when they arrived

One day, a woman
Who seemed to see him too
Started walking to him
His dream had come true
Her smile somehow held him
Like it knew his name
The one he couldn't say to others
Walking through his planes
When they met at last
Happy not the word
So quickly their forever
His voice finally heard
She explained with no sadness
How fast their time would pass
"Save tomorrow for me
I will always come back"

# 13. Not A Drop To Drink

Weve been thirsty
But there is no rain
So much longing
So much pain
Tears barely fall
In this desert sun
Away water is called
For when there is none
Not we survive
The hells that we make
And damned how try
But the men have turned fake
No world that is true
No river can flow
Everything we lose
And no where to go
Prayer and dances
A new weatherman
No water can fall
On this starving land

The well has run dry
The pipes filled with rust
So we soak up the tears
Until we turn to dust

# 14. Thirsty

Drink

Sate you thirst

Were hot

Parched

This may be our last chance

We have wandered far

Water

Water

Water

The only life we have left in this stream

So drink

Be filled

# 15. A Sailor for my Seas

A daughter
A blessing
The universe with a cute pink bow
Everything
Love
Hope
Tomorrows promised
But still
A wild being
Ultraviolence
A new creature for a new world
A daughter in this time, a challenge
How I met my darkness
And oh the depths
Thank heaven for little girls
Thank the hells for the light
May she shine and be seen and be loved
May her name be known
My Aurora
My wave of majestic light

Who wore the bows
Who danced in the shows
And whose rage I find beautiful
She will endure
And I in her
I am ever so thankful

# 16. The Freeze

Cold winds are coming
To follow the flames
Our new world was burning
It won't be the same
To hot for this city
Built of paper and sticks
Nothing but kindling
And hearts that grew sick
I pray we allow
What we often not
Coldness to dwell
Though some like it hot
For me myself
I can't wait to chill
These flames, though exciting
Are here for the kill
The ice and snow
And cold winter wind
Will call us all home
To begin again

Next year we spring forth
But lets enjoy our time
If you need get your blanket
I will not need mine
My soul still aflame
From fuel not yet spent
My journey in waiting
For new life to begin
I need this cold air
We need the refresh
Time to feel cool
And catch our breath

# 17. Reign

Of Satan and seasons
Of God and the wind
Of ancients and demons
Of foes and best friends
Of reason and truth
Of sickness and lies
Of hatred and love
Of nothing but time
A storm of the mind
That can bow and break
A mystery and puzzle
That can make the Earth shake
A perfected design
For each breath you take
An intentional harm
To end all of this
A well-timed sacrifice
We payed for with bliss
A lie we were sold
Sealed with a kiss

Tomorrow forgotten
The past faded away
The here and the now
Too dark to say
We wander out far
Hoping there is a way
Even with light
And shadows that care
There is no way out
Our prison is here
Caged by our minds
And delirious fear
In with the criminals
To pick all the locks
They glow in the darkness
Like all the clocks
Pirates set sail from
Deepest of docks
Run lovely ones
Run and be free
Tomorrow forgotten
For new things to see
Run out past sunset
In to new dreams

# 18. Watering the Garden

Tell me something universe
For I seek to know
The truth that I've been hiding from
I'm bored of lies we're told
Tell what the stars mean
Tell me why I'm here
Tell of the gods of old
Tell me more of fear
The wind whispered in my ear
The cows gazed upon me whole
The babies told me everything
The river touched my soul
I can call on anything
To share this life with me
Pray they accept this offering
Of what it is to me
A dance of light and wondering
And imagined wondrous thing
The darkness climbing inward
To show what it can bring

The beings in the shadows
And ones of dazzling light
The loveliest of humans
And ones that like to fight
Gathered here together
In the wandered mind
Treasures I have collected
To know each of these kinds
I even loved the wildest
Places my mind roamed
I am thankful for each family
Sharing places known
Now settled back in my today
I imagine my home world
Begin the sharing of my journey
With some heaven's little girl
Her life passing through me
My daughter but yet not
The treasure I was given
From a land that time forgot

# 19. Dark River

There is a pain I once knew
That should not exist
Cruel
Sharp and hollow
Eternal
Unbearable
Time heals all wounds
But not this
Time knows not this
Also cannot bear it
Best it can do is lie
Cover it
Never tell a soul
It told one once
No cuts
No bruises
No scars
All encompassing
A tough pill one cannot swallow
But it passes through me still

Years and years have passed
But it is known
And will be known
No where to place this
I cannot let it leave
This should touch no other
I pray they do not look
Fear has left
I drank this pain and it is me now
I love it
I love that it came to me to see it
To know
To hold
I won't ask why
I know who I am
These things find me
May it never be true
This pain
May it lay as an imaginary line
One day we may not need to be reminded
Maybe it will leave when someone else can gather it
Or perhaps this dies with me
I leave it unwatered yet it remains just as sharp
An eternal suffering
Not meant for human
Not meant to be known
May it fall asleep

May we fall asleep
To dream of gentler things than the horrors of hell
Bombarding
Relentless
May our souls bring each other peace
That when cruelty finds us
We can escape

# 20. Time Washes Away

We were to know each other here
But the world swept us away
Chores to do, places to go
And of course bills to pay
I find you in the spaces lost
To time that fades away
Hands to hold, stories to share
Games we didn't play
Could've, would've, should've
Things to which we cling
The love was ours, we it slip
Down into the drain
What we couldn't share at home
We imagine, time to time
A world that we could not afford
That I still know is mine
I watch as the Earth drifts away
From all that could have been
I wish I owned the universe
I'd write our story once again

# 21. Undertow

I drown now
All that I was milled into the sea
I can swim but the current is strong
I am not afraid
What I was, nothing more or less than what I will
become
But oh the difference
I will ever know
Even if no one else does
What lies in that change
Change to bear
Change to spend
Change that leaves a heart aching for what was
Unable to claim what was promised
Alone
But alive
Drowning